Apple Vision Pro Mastery

The Comprehensive User Guide

William C. Wills

© **2024 by William C. Wills.** *All rights reserved. No part of this publication may be reproduced, distributed, or transmitted in any form or by any means, including photocopying, recording, or other electronic or mechanical methods, without the prior written permission of the publisher, except in the case of brief quotations embodied in critical reviews and certain other noncommercial uses permitted by copyright law.*

Table of Contents

Introduction -- 4

Chapter 1
Unveiling the Vision Pro -------------------------- 10

   History and Evolution of Apple Vision Pro --------- 10

   Overview of Features and Capabilities --------------- 12

Chapter 2
Setting Up Your Vision Pro ----------------------- 15

   Unboxing and Initial Setup -------------------------- 15

   Installing Necessary Software and Updates --------- 17

   Customizing Settings for Optimal Use --------------- 20

Chapter 3
Navigating the Interface -------------------------- 23

   Understanding the User Interface and Controls -- 23

   Mastering Touch Gestures and Voice Commands - 25

   Personalizing Your Display and Accessibility Options --- 27

Chapter 4
Advanced Features and Functions --------------- 31

   Exploring Advanced Camera and Imaging Capabilities --- 31

   Utilizing AI and Machine Learning Features ------ 33

Integrating with Other Apple Devices and Services --- 36

Chapter 5
Troubleshooting and Support ------------------- 39
Common Issues and How to Resolve Them -------- 39

Accessing Apple Support and Community Forums 41

Maintaining and Updating Your Device ------------ 44

Chapter 6
Vision Pro in Professional Use ------------------ 47
Case Studies: How Professionals Are Using Vision Pro --- 47

Tips for Integrating Vision Pro into Your Workflow -- 49

Chapter 7
The Future of Vision Pro -------------------------- 53
Upcoming Features and Updates -------------------- 53

The Role of Vision Pro in the Future of Technology --- 56

Conclusion --- 60
Appendices --- 65
About the Author --- 70

Introduction

The Apple Vision Pro is a cutting-edge wearable device that integrates augmented reality (AR) and virtual reality (VR), providing users with an unparalleled immersive computing experience. Introduced by Apple in 2024, the Vision Pro symbolizes a groundbreaking shift in technology interaction, blurring the boundaries between the digital and physical spheres.

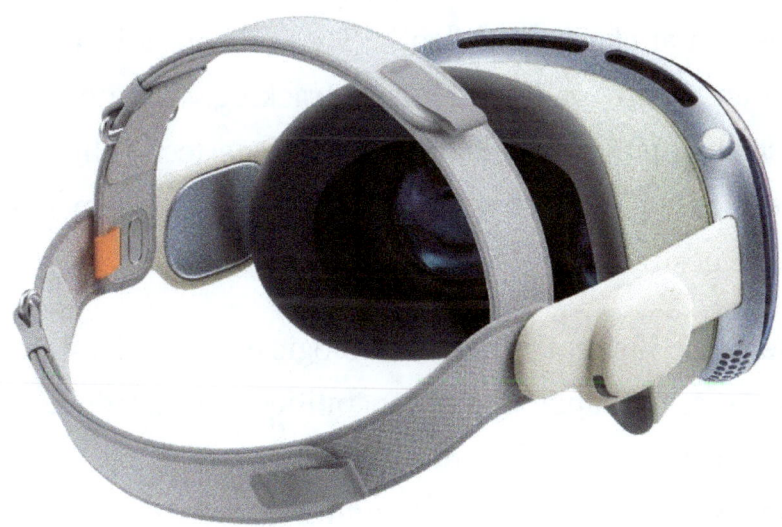

At the core of the Vision Pro lies Apple's state-of-the-art spatial computing technology, which seamlessly integrates advanced sensors, powerful processors, and innovative optics. This groundbreaking system enables the device to create highly realistic and responsive augmented and virtual reality environments, projecting virtual objects and information directly into the user's field of view.

This cutting-edge technology offers a multitude of possibilities for businesses and academics to explore and leverage, providing new and exciting ways to create immersive and engaging experiences for their users.

The Vision Pro features two high-resolution displays, one for each eye, delivering stunning visuals with exceptional clarity and depth. These displays work in tandem with advanced eye-tracking technology, ensuring that virtual elements remain perfectly aligned and focused, regardless of the user's head movements or eye positions.

The Apple Vision Pro is a technological innovation that boasts remarkable visual capabilities. In addition, it incorporates spatial audio technology that provides users with a fully immersive auditory experience.

The technology enables sound to be precisely mapped and rendered in three-dimensional space, creating a profound sense of presence and realism that enhances the overall immersive experience. With the integration of spatial audio technology, the Apple Vision Pro elevates the standard of immersive technology to new heights.

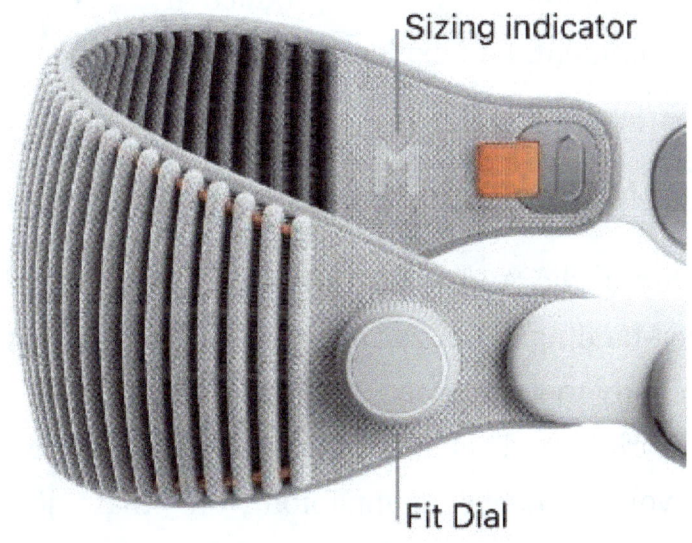
Sizing indicator
Fit Dial

With a sleek and ergonomic design, the Vision Pro is both comfortable and lightweight, allowing for extended wear during work, entertainment, or creative sessions. Its advanced hand-tracking system and intuitive gesture controls enable natural and intuitive interactions with virtual objects and user interfaces, making the device feel like an extension of the user's own body and mind.

The true power of the Apple Vision Pro lies in its versatility. It transitions between AR and VR modes, enabling users to seamlessly blend digital content with their physical surroundings or be fully immersed in virtual environments. This flexibility opens up a world of possibilities for productivity, creativity, entertainment, and exploration, redefining the way we work, learn, and play.

How this Book will Help You Master the Device

Mastering the Apple Vision Pro requires not only an understanding of its cutting-edge technology but also the ability to seamlessly integrate it into your daily life and workflows. This comprehensive guide is designed to be your trusted companion on that journey, empowering you to unlock the full potential of this revolutionary device.

Within the pages of this book, you will find a wealth of knowledge and practical insights that will take you from a beginner's understanding to an expert-level mastery of the Apple Vision Pro. Through clear and concise explanations, step-by-step instructions, and real-world examples, you will gain a deep understanding of the device's capabilities, features, and nuances.

From setting up your Apple Vision Pro and navigating its intuitive user interface to exploring the boundless possibilities of augmented reality (AR) and virtual reality (VR) experiences, this guide will be your constant companion. You will learn how to leverage the device's advanced hand-tracking and gesture controls to interact with virtual objects and environments in natural and intuitive ways, blurring the lines between the physical and digital realms.

Whether you're a professional seeking to enhance your productivity and collaboration efforts, a creative individual looking to unleash your artistic vision, or an entertainment enthusiast eager to immerse yourself in mind-bending virtual worlds, this book has something for everyone. It will equip you with the knowledge and skills necessary to harness the full power of the Apple Vision Pro for your specific needs and goals.

From productivity tips and tricks to advanced customization techniques, from exploring the vast ecosystem of apps and experiences to developing your own AR/VR content (for those with a developer's mindset), this guide will leave no stone unturned. It will empower you to seamlessly integrate the Apple Vision Pro into your daily life, maximizing its potential and unlocking new levels of efficiency, creativity, and immersion.

With this comprehensive user guide by your side, you will embark on a journey of mastery, transforming the way you perceive and interact with technology. Whether you're a seasoned tech enthusiast or a newcomer to the world of spatial computing, this book will be your trusted companion, ensuring that you fully harness the power and potential of the Apple Vision Pro.

Chapter 1

Unveiling the Vision Pro

History and Evolution of Apple Vision Pro

The journey of Apple Vision Pro began long before its public unveiling, rooted in Apple's consistent pursuit of innovation. The seeds for what would become Vision Pro were planted with the acquisition of the German augmented reality company Metaio in 2015. This strategic move hinted at Apple's interest in the augmented reality (AR) space, which would later culminate in the development of the Vision Pro.

By 2023, Apple had made significant strides in AR technology, leveraging its expertise in hardware and software to create a seamless mixed-reality experience. The announcement of the Apple Vision Pro headset at the Worldwide Developers Conference was the culmination of years of speculation, rumors, and technological development.

The Vision Pro represented a significant leap forward in Apple's product line, being the first major new product category since the Apple Watch in 2015. It was marketed as a "spatial computer," integrating digital media with the natural world in a way that had never been done before. The device's capabilities were vast, allowing for interaction through motion gestures, eye tracking, and speech recognition, all powered by the custom-designed visionOS.

Apple's long-term vision for the Vision Pro is not just about the device itself but how it integrates into a broader ecosystem of products and services. The technology that powers the Vision Pro is expected to pave the way for future innovations, including the much-anticipated Apple Car. The Vision Pro's AR technology could enhance the driving experience by providing information directly within the driver's line of sight.

The Vision Pro's release in February 2024 marked a new era for Apple, one that promises to redefine our interaction with technology. As we look back at the history and evolution of the Apple Vision Pro, we can appreciate the meticulous planning, innovation, and execution that Apple is renowned for. The Vision Pro is not just a product; it's a vision of the future, a testament to Apple's commitment to pushing the boundaries of what's possible.

Overview of Features and Capabilities

The Apple Vision Pro stands as a testament to Apple's commitment to innovation, merging the physical and digital worlds in a way that redefines our interaction with technology. Here is an overview of its most notable features and capabilities:

Spatial Computing Powerhouse
- At the heart of the Vision Pro is the R1 chip, designed to deliver a virtually lag-free, real-time view of the world. This chip powers the ultra-high-resolution display system, which boasts 23 million pixels across two displays—providing more than a 4K TV's worth of resolution for each eye.

Apps and Desktop Freedom
- Vision Pro introduces an infinite canvas for your apps, allowing you to arrange and scale them freely in your space. This spatial arrangement of

apps like Safari, Notes, and Messages transforms how you interact with your favorite software, offering a new level of multitasking and productivity.

Entertainment Anywhere
- Transform any room into a personal theater with Vision Pro. Movies, shows, and games can be expanded to your preferred size, complemented by Spatial Audio for an immersive experience. The high-resolution displays ensure stunning content quality, whether you're on a flight or lounging at home.

Photography and Videography Reimagined
- Vision Pro is Apple's first 3D camera, allowing you to capture spatial photos and videos. Relive your memories in 3D with immersive Spatial Audio and view your existing photo and video library at an unprecedented scale. Panoramas wrap around you, placing you back in the moment of capture.

Enhanced Connectivity
- The device revolutionizes meetings and collaborations. FaceTime video tiles are life-size, expanding as more participants join. Within

FaceTime, you can use apps to work on documents together, making remote work more engaging and efficient.

Intuitive Design

- Decades of design experience have culminated in the Vision Pro's elegant form. A singular piece of laminated glass acts as an optical surface for the cameras and sensors, while a custom aluminum alloy frame ensures comfort and durability.

VisionOS: A New Dimension of Interaction

- Built upon the foundations of macOS, iOS, and iPadOS, visionOS is Apple's first spatial operating system. Control the Vision Pro with your eyes, hands, and voice for intuitive and magical interactions. Look to select, tap your fingers to activate, and use the virtual keyboard or dictation for input.

The Apple Vision Pro is not just a new device; it's a new way of experiencing the world. With its advanced features and capabilities, it promises to unlock new possibilities for creativity, productivity, and entertainment.

Chapter 2

Setting Up Your Vision Pro

Unboxing and Initial Setup

Welcome to the world of Apple Vision Pro, where your journey into augmented reality begins. Here's how to get started:

Unboxing Your Vision Pro
- Begin by carefully removing the sleek packaging of your Apple Vision Pro. Inside, you'll find the Vision Pro headset, a precision-crafted piece of technology designed for an unparalleled AR experience.
- Lift the device from its protective casing and gently set it on a flat surface. The battery pack, which powers the headset, is tethered to a cord for easy charging.

- Accompanying the headset is the Vision Pro Travel Case and a set of Zeiss lens inserts, which ensure your Vision Pro is protected and customized for your vision needs.

Initial Setup

- Charge your Vision Pro using the included battery pack. A full charge is recommended before first use to ensure uninterrupted setup and exploration.
- Power on your Vision Pro by pressing the button located on the side of the headset. You'll be greeted by a welcome screen and guided through the initial setup process.
- Connect your Vision Pro to your Apple ID and Wi-Fi network. This will allow you to access the full suite of features and synchronize with your other Apple devices.

- Adjust the Zeiss lens inserts if necessary, ensuring a comfortable fit and clear vision. The Vision Pro is designed to accommodate a wide range of vision preferences.
- Explore the tutorial provided by visionOS, which will introduce you to the basics of navigation and interaction within the AR environment.

By adhering to these instructions, your Apple Vision Pro will be equipped to transport you to a new realm of computing where the digital and physical worlds converge seamlessly. Enjoy the journey!

Installing Necessary Software and Updates

To ensure your Apple Vision Pro operates at peak performance, installing the latest software and updates is crucial. Here's a step-by-step guide to help you through the process:

Checking for Updates
- Upon initial setup, your Vision Pro will automatically check for the latest version of visionOS.

- To manually check for updates, navigate to the **Settings** menu, select **General**, and then tap on **Software Update**.

Installing Software

- If an update is available, you'll see an **Install Now** button. Tap it to begin the installation process.
- Your Vision Pro will download the update and prompt you to install it. During this time, ensure your device is connected to a power source to prevent any interruptions.

Updating Apps

- Open the **App Store** on your Vision Pro and tap on the **Updates** tab.
- Here, you'll find a list of apps with available updates. Tap **Update All** to refresh all your apps, or select individual apps to update them one by one.

Restarting Your Device

- After installing updates, your Vision Pro may restart automatically. If it doesn't, you can manually restart it by holding down the power button and selecting **Restart**.

- Once your Vision Pro reboots, it will be up-to-date with the latest features and security enhancements.

Setting Up Automatic Updates
- To automate future updates, go back to the **Software Update** settings and toggle on **Automatic Updates**.
- With this feature enabled, your Vision Pro will keep itself updated without requiring manual intervention.

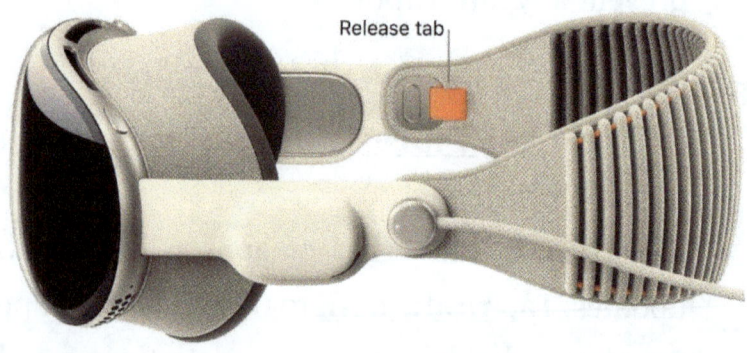

By keeping your Apple Vision Pro updated, you ensure access to the latest features, improvements, and security patches, which will provide you with the best possible augmented reality experience.

Customizing Settings for Optimal Use

To tailor your Apple Vision Pro for the best personal experience, customizing its settings is key. Here's how to optimize your device for your unique needs:

Personalizing Your Vision Pro
- Begin by accessing the **Settings** menu, where you'll find a plethora of options to personalize your device.
- Adjust the **Display & Brightness** settings to find the perfect balance for your eyes. You can set the brightness level, choose a color scheme, and even schedule dark mode to reduce eye strain during evening hours.

Enhancing the Audio Experience
- Dive into the **Sounds & Haptics** settings to customize audio feedback. You can adjust the volume of alerts, enable spatial audio, and fine-tune the intensity of haptic feedback to match your preferences.

Optimizing Interaction
- The **Accessibility** settings offer a range of features to make your Vision Pro more user-friendly. Options like voice control, motion

reduction, and touch accommodations ensure that interacting with your device is a smooth experience.

Securing Your Device

Security is paramount, so head over to **Privacy & Security** settings. Here, you can manage app permissions, enable location services, and set up Face ID for secure and effortless authentication.

Staying Connected

In the **Wi-Fi & Bluetooth** settings, ensure your Vision Pro is always connected to your preferred networks and devices. You can also manage your cellular settings if you're using a model with mobile connectivity.

Managing Notifications

To avoid distractions, tailor your **Notifications** settings. Choose which apps can send you alerts and customize how these notifications are displayed and sounded.

Conserving Battery Life

The **Battery** settings provide insights into your usage patterns and offer recommendations for conserving power. You can also enable low-power mode to extend battery life when needed.

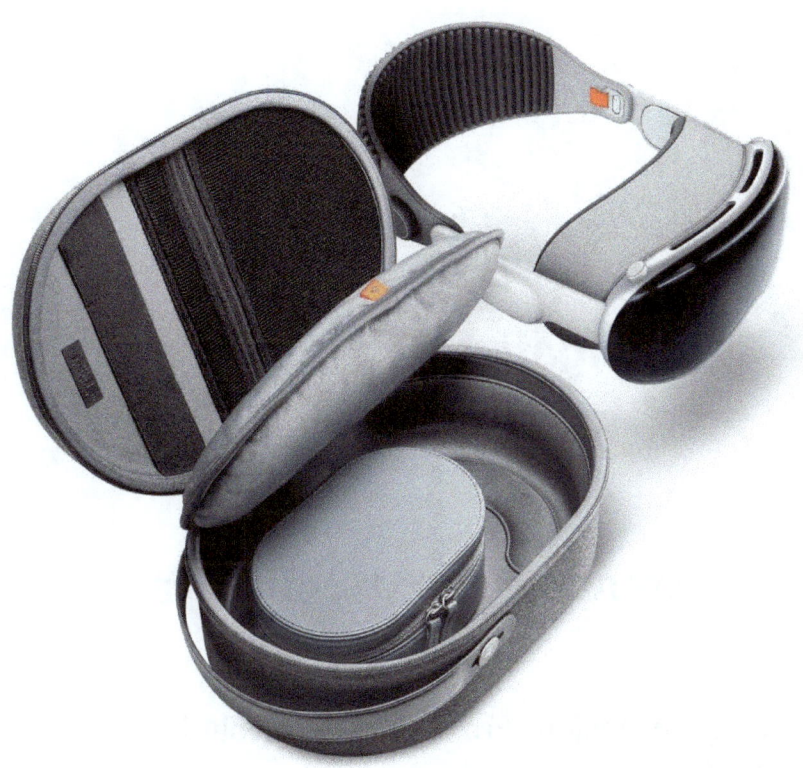

By customizing these settings, you can ensure that your Apple Vision Pro works just the way you want it to, enhancing both your productivity and enjoyment.

Chapter 3

Navigating the Interface

Understanding the User Interface and Controls

The Apple Vision Pro offers a revolutionary user interface that is intuitive and seamless, blending the physical and digital worlds. Here's a guide to understanding the interface and mastering the controls:

The Vision Pro Interface
- The interface of the Vision Pro is a spatial environment where applications and information are displayed in a three-dimensional space around you.
- You can interact with your environment using natural gestures, voice commands, and eye movements, making the experience fluid and natural.

Control Center

- The Control Center is your hub for quick access to essential controls and features. To open it, look up and tap near the top of your view.
- In the Control Center, you can manage settings like volume, brightness, and connectivity and access features like Guest User and Travel Mode.

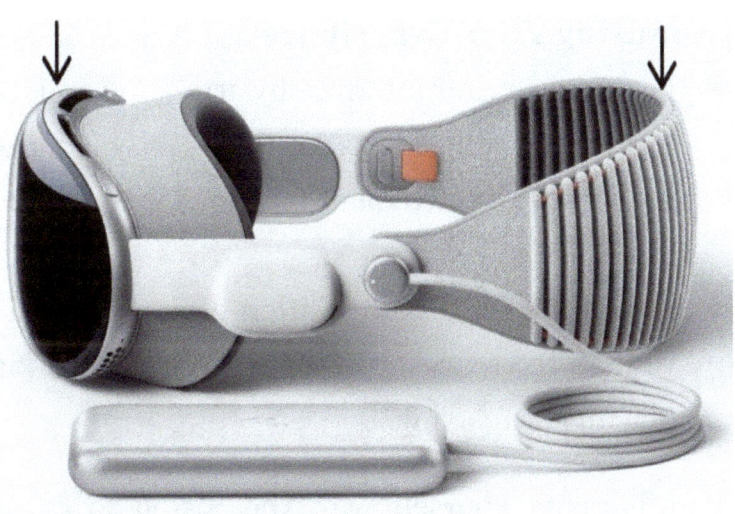

Vision Pro Keyboard

- The Vision Pro keyboard is a virtual input device that appears when you need to type. It tracks your hand movements and finger taps, allowing for a tactile typing experience in a virtual space.
- You can also use voice dictation or the gaze-and-blink method for hands-free typing, providing flexibility in how you input text.

Navigating Apps and Content
- To navigate between apps and content, use your eyes to look at what you want to select and perform a simple gesture to activate it.
- The Vision Pro's interface is designed to be context-aware, bringing relevant information and controls to the forefront as needed.

Customizing Your Experience
- Personalize your interface by arranging apps and widgets in your space. You can pin your most-used apps in convenient locations, making them easily accessible.
- Adjust the scale and position of displays to suit your preferences, whether you're working, playing, or relaxing.

By familiarizing yourself with the Vision Pro's user interface and controls, you'll unlock the full potential of this cutting-edge device, enhancing your interaction with technology and the world around you.

Mastering Touch Gestures and Voice Commands

The Apple Vision Pro introduces a suite of intuitive touch gestures and voice commands that redefine interaction with technology. Here's how to master these controls for a seamless experience:

Touch Gestures
- **Tap:** Select options and open apps by looking at the content and tapping your index finger and thumb together.
- **Touch:** Interact directly with elements, such as typing on the virtual keyboard, by touching keys with your fingers.
- **Pinch and Hold:** Show additional options or zoom in and out by pinching and holding your thumb and index finger together.
- **Pinch and Drag:** Move windows, scroll through content, or drag objects by pinching and holding them and then dragging them to the desired location.
- **Swipe:** Scroll quickly through content by pinching and flicking your wrist.

Voice Commands
- **Siri:** Activate Siri for hands-free assistance. Say, "Hey Siri," followed by your request.
- **Dictation:** Enter text using dictation. Tap the microphone icon on the virtual keyboard and speak your text aloud.

- **Accessibility Commands:** Use specialized voice commands to interact with your Vision Pro's accessibility features.

Using the Digital Crown and Top Button
- **Home View:** Press the Digital Crown to return to the Home View.
- **Recenter Content:** Press and hold the Digital Crown to recenter your content within your view.
- **Adjust Volume:** Turn the Digital Crown to adjust the immersion or volume levels.
- **Capture Mode:** Press the top button to open Capture for spatial photos and videos.
- **Force Quit:** Simultaneously press and hold the top button and Digital Crown to force quit applications.

By familiarizing yourself with these gestures and commands, you can navigate and control your Apple Vision Pro with confidence and ease, making the most of its advanced capabilities.

Personalizing Your Display and Accessibility Options

The Apple Vision Pro is designed with inclusivity in mind, offering a range of customization options to cater to your individual preferences and needs. Here's how to personalize your display and accessibility settings:

Adjusting Display Settings
- Navigate to **Settings > Display & Brightness** to adjust the visual aspects of your Vision Pro. Here, you can modify the brightness, text size, and color settings to suit your visual comfort.
- For those who prefer larger text, the **Zoom** feature allows you to magnify the screen or specific areas, making it easier to read and interact with content.

Enhancing Visual Accessibility
- The **VoiceOver** feature provides auditory descriptions of what's on your screen, ideal for users who are blind or have low vision. It can be turned on by triple-clicking the Digital Crown.
- The **Magnifier** works as a digital magnifying glass, using the camera to increase the size of physical objects for better visibility on your screen.

Customizing Audio and Haptic Feedback
- In **Settings > Sounds & Haptics,** you can personalize audio cues and haptic feedback to match your experience of sound and touch.

- Adjust the balance and mono audio settings to accommodate hearing differences, ensuring that you receive clear and balanced audio feedback.

Configuring Eye Input and Motion

- For those with specific vision prescriptions or conditions, **Settings > Accessibility > Eye Input** allows you to customize which eye controls the Vision Pro, enhancing comfort and accuracy.
- To reduce motion effects or stabilize display changes, visit **Settings > Accessibility > Motion** to toggle on features like **Reduce Motion** or **Ignore Eye Movements to Stabilize**.

Utilizing AssistiveTouch and Dwell Control

- **AssistiveTouch** helps users with physical and motor challenges by providing alternative ways to interact with the Vision Pro, such as customizable gestures and actions.
- **Dwell Control** allows you to perform actions by simply dwelling (resting) your gaze on interface elements, reducing the need for physical interaction.

Leveraging Switch Control and Voice Commands

- **Switch Control** enables users with limited mobility to navigate the Vision Pro using a variety of adaptive switches and devices.
- With **Voice Control,** you can navigate and interact with your Vision Pro using just your voice, providing a hands-free experience.

By personalizing your display and accessibility options, you can create an experience that is tailored to your unique way of interacting with technology, making the Apple Vision Pro a device that truly adapts to you.

Chapter 4

Advanced Features and Functions

Exploring Advanced Camera and Imaging Capabilities

The Apple Vision Pro is not just a leap into augmented reality; it's a foray into advanced photography and videography. With its sophisticated camera system, the Vision Pro redefines the art of capturing moments. Here's an exploration of its advanced camera and imaging capabilities:

A New Dimension in Photography
- The Vision Pro features **two high-resolution main cameras** that allow users to capture spatial photos in stunning detail.
- These cameras are designed to work in tandem with the device's spatial computing power,

enabling you to take pictures that are rich in depth and texture.

Revolutionary 3D Camera System
- As Apple's first 3D camera, the Vision Pro lets you record spatial videos that you can relive with a sense of presence and immersion, thanks to the **Spatial Audio** technology.
- The device's camera system includes **six world-facing tracking cameras, four eye-tracking cameras,** a **TrueDepth camera,** and a **LiDAR Scanner.** This array of sensors ensures that every photo and video you take is not just a memory but an experience.

Immersive Content Creation
- The Vision Pro's imaging capabilities extend beyond traditional photography, allowing users to create content that's ready for the next generation of media consumption.
- Whether you're a professional content creator or an enthusiast, the Vision Pro's cameras offer a new canvas for your creativity.

Seamless Integration with iPhone
- The Vision Pro's cameras are complemented by the ability to take spatial videos with the **iPhone**

15 Pro and then view them on the Vision Pro in a fully immersive manner.
- This integration ensures that your content creation workflow is uninterrupted and that your creations are displayed at the highest quality.

Advanced Sensors for Real-Time Feedback
- The Vision Pro's camera system is supported by **four inertial measurement units (IMUs),** a **flicker sensor,** and an **ambient light sensor.** These sensors provide real-time feedback to the device, ensuring that your photos and videos are perfectly captured, no matter the environment.

By harnessing the advanced camera and imaging capabilities of the Apple Vision Pro, users can capture and create content that's not only visually stunning but also rich in depth and context, offering a glimpse into the future of photography and videography.

Utilizing AI and Machine Learning Features

The Apple Vision Pro harnesses the power of AI and machine learning to deliver a truly personalized and intelligent user experience. Here's an insight into how these technologies are integrated into the device:

Intelligent FaceTime Avatars
- Using **advanced machine learning,** Vision Pro can create hyper-realistic digital avatars during FaceTime calls.
- The device scans your face with front-facing cameras to generate a 3D likeness that captures your true expressions, allowing for more engaging and realistic video chats.

Adaptive User Interface
- Vision Pro's interface is dynamic and context-aware, thanks to machine learning algorithms that anticipate your needs and preferences.
- The system adapts in real-time, bringing relevant information and controls to the forefront and enhancing usability and efficiency.

Enhanced Spatial Awareness
- Machine learning is also at the core of Vision Pro's spatial awareness capabilities. It enables the device to understand and interact with the physical environment more naturally and intuitively.
- This technology allows for precise tracking and placement of digital content within your space, making AR experiences more immersive and realistic.

Personalized Content Recommendations
- Vision Pro leverages AI to provide personalized content recommendations based on your usage patterns and preferences.
- Whether it's suggesting apps, media, or activities, the device learns from your behavior to offer tailored experiences that resonate with your interests.

Voice and Gesture Recognition
- The device's AI capabilities extend to recognizing and interpreting voice commands and hand gestures.
- This allows for a seamless interaction where the device understands and responds to your commands accurately and efficiently.

Proactive Support and Maintenance
- Vision Pro's machine learning systems monitor device performance and health, proactively identifying issues and offering solutions.
- This ensures that your device remains in optimal condition, providing support and updates as needed.

By integrating AI and machine learning, the Apple Vision Pro not only enhances current functionalities but also paves the way for future innovations that will continue to transform our interaction with technology.

Integrating with Other Apple Devices and Services

The Apple Vision Pro is not an island unto itself; it is a part of the extensive Apple ecosystem, designed to work in harmony with your other Apple devices and services. Here's how the Vision Pro integrates seamlessly into the Apple family:

Seamless Synchronization
- With **iCloud,** your photos, documents, and other data are synchronized across all your devices, including the Vision Pro.
- Your content is always up-to-date and accessible, whether you're using an iPhone, iPad, Mac, or Vision Pro.

Continuity and Handoff
- Start an activity on one device and pick it up on another with **Continuity.** The Vision Pro supports Handoff for apps like Mail, Safari, Pages, Numbers, Keynote, Maps, Messages, Reminders, Calendar, and Contacts.

- This feature ensures that your workflow is uninterrupted, no matter which device you're using.

Universal Clipboard
- Copy text, images, or video on one Apple device and paste it onto another, including the Vision Pro. This **Universal Clipboard** feature makes moving content between devices effortless.

AirPlay
- With **AirPlay,** you can stream music, videos, and more from your Vision Pro to your Apple TV or AirPlay 2-compatible smart TV.
- Share your experiences on a bigger screen with ease, and enjoy content with family and friends.

FaceTime and Messages
- Stay connected with friends and family using **FaceTime** and **Messages.** The Vision Pro brings these services to life in new ways, offering immersive communication experiences.
- Engage in life-size video calls or send interactive messages that leverage the spatial capabilities of the Vision Pro.

Apple Music and Podcasts

- Access your **Apple Music** library and listen to your favorite tunes or podcasts on the Vision Pro.
- The spatial audio capabilities of the Vision Pro provide an extraordinary listening experience that's rich and immersive.

Find My

- Keep track of your Vision Pro alongside your other Apple devices using the **Find My** app.
- If your Vision Pro is misplaced, you can play a sound to locate it or use the map to find its last known location.

Health Integration

- The Vision Pro contributes to your **Health** data by tracking your activities and workouts, adding a new dimension to your health and fitness journey.
- Monitor your progress and stay motivated with insights that span across your devices.

By integrating with other Apple devices and services, the Apple Vision Pro enriches the Apple ecosystem, providing a cohesive and connected experience that enhances your digital life.

Chapter 5

Troubleshooting and Support

Common Issues and How to Resolve Them

The Apple Vision Pro is a sophisticated piece of technology, but like any device, it may encounter issues. Here's a guide to some common problems and their resolutions:

Issue: Light Leakage
- Some users have reported light leaking through the bottom of the headset, especially noticeable in dark environments.
- **Resolution:** Ensure that the Vision Pro is updated with the latest software, as updates may help reduce this issue. Check the fit of the Light Seal and adjust the cushioning to ensure it makes proper contact with your face. If the problem

persists, consider visiting an Apple Store for a fitting adjustment or replacement.

Issue: Audio Problems

- Reports include the right speaker pod overheating, sound not emitting from one or both speakers and low volume when using Bluetooth earphones.
- **Resolution:** Disconnect the battery pack when not in use to prevent overheating. If there's no sound, check for debris blocking the speaker arm contact, clean it, and reattach the strap. For low-volume issues, ensure that your Bluetooth device is properly paired and the volume is appropriately adjusted.

Issue: Spontaneous Cracking

- Some users have noticed cracks developing on their Vision Pro, particularly from the top to the bottom of the headset.
- **Resolution:** This may be a manufacturing defect. If you notice such cracking, contact Apple Support or visit an Apple Store for an assessment and potential replacement.

Issue: Eye Tracking and Glare

- Difficulties with eye tracking and persistent glare have been reported, especially in low-light conditions.
- **Resolution:** Regularly clean the lenses and ensure that the headset's software is up-to-date. If issues with eye tracking persist, recalibrate the eye-tracking feature through the settings menu.

Issue: Hardware/Software Malfunctions
- Users may encounter various hardware or software issues, ranging from unresponsive controls to system errors.
- **Resolution:** Restart your Vision Pro to resolve temporary glitches. For persistent problems, reset your device to factory settings or seek assistance from Apple Support.

Regular maintenance and software updates can prevent many common problems and ensure your Vision Pro remains in top condition.

Accessing Apple Support and Community Forums

When you need assistance with your Apple Vision Pro, Apple's support and community forums are invaluable resources. Here's how to navigate these platforms for help and advice:

Apple Support Community

- The **Apple Support Community** is a place where you can find answers, ask questions, and connect with other Apple Vision Pro users.
- To access the community, visit the Apple Support website and navigate to the community section dedicated to the Vision Pro.
- Search for existing discussions that might address your concerns, or start a new thread to seek help from fellow users and Apple experts.

MacRumors Forums

- The **MacRumors Forums** offer a platform for users to discuss their experiences, share tips, and troubleshoot issues related to the Vision Pro.
- Engage in conversations about the latest updates, features, and accessories, and gain insights from a community of enthusiasts and professionals.

Reddit Community

- **Reddit** hosts a subreddit specifically for the Apple Vision Pro, where members post news, reviews, and discussions about the device.

- This community is a great place to stay updated on the latest trends, find solutions to common problems, and share your Vision Pro experiences.

Direct Apple Support
- For personalized support, you can contact Apple directly through their website or the Apple Support app.
- Apple offers various support options, including live chat, phone calls, or scheduling an appointment at an Apple Store or authorized service provider.

Utilizing Online Resources
- Apple's online support also includes detailed articles, guides, and tutorials that can help you resolve many common issues.
- The **Apple Vision Pro User Guide** is a comprehensive resource that covers everything from setup to advanced features.

By leveraging these support and community forums, you can find the help you need to enjoy a seamless experience with your Apple Vision Pro.

Maintaining and Updating Your Device

Keeping your Apple Vision Pro well-maintained and updated is essential for optimal performance. Here's a guide to help you keep your device in top condition:

Regular Maintenance
- Clean your Vision Pro regularly with a soft, lint-free cloth to remove dust and fingerprints.
- Inspect the lenses for smudges or debris, as these can affect the clarity of your AR experience. Use a microfiber cloth and a lens cleaning solution if necessary.
- Check the fit and condition of the head strap and cushioning periodically, replacing them if they show signs of wear.

Updating VisionOS
- Keeping your Vision Pro updated with the latest version of visionOS ensures you have the newest features and security enhancements.

- To update automatically, go to **Settings > General > Software Update > Automatic Updates** and turn on **VisionOS Updates.**
- For manual updates, navigate to **Settings > General > Software Update.** If an update is available, tap **Download and Install** or **Install Now.**
- During the update process, you'll see a progress bar on the front display. Ensure your device has sufficient charge or is connected to power before updating.

Backing Up Your Data
- It's crucial to back up your Vision Pro regularly. You can set up automatic backups to iCloud or perform manual backups through the settings menu.
- In case of any issues, having a backup allows you to restore your device to its previous state without losing your data.

Battery Care
- To maximize battery lifespan, avoid exposing your Vision Pro to extreme temperatures.
- Charge the battery pack using the provided charger and cable, and disconnect it once fully charged to prevent overcharging.

Software Health Checks

- Use the built-in diagnostics in visionOS to check for software issues. These tools can help identify and resolve problems quickly.
- If you encounter persistent issues, consider resetting your Vision Pro to factory settings as a last resort.

By following this maintenance and updating guidelines, you can ensure that your Apple Vision Pro remains a reliable and high-performing device for all your augmented reality needs.

Chapter 6

Vision Pro in Professional Use

Case Studies: How Professionals Are Using Vision Pro

The Apple Vision Pro has transcended the boundaries of personal entertainment and gaming, finding its place in various professional domains. Here are some case studies that illustrate the impact of Vision Pro in professional settings:

Case Study 1: Productivity and Workspace Transformation

- Professionals across industries have adopted Vision Pro to create virtual workspaces. With the ability to open multiple screens simultaneously and organize them within a virtual space, the Vision Pro has enhanced productivity by enabling multitasking in an immersive environment.

Case Study 2: AI-Powered Spatial Banking

- In the financial sector, Vision Pro is being used to revolutionize customer experiences through AI-powered spatial banking. This next-generation banking experience leverages artificial intelligence for hyper-personalization, providing customers with tailored financial advice and services.

Case Study 3: Healthcare and Telemedicine

- Vision Pro's advanced imaging and spatial computing capabilities are being utilized in healthcare for remote diagnostics and telemedicine. Doctors can conduct virtual consultations with patients, providing a more interactive and personal level of care.

Case Study 4: Education and Virtual Learning

- Educators are using Vision Pro to create immersive learning experiences. The device's spatial features allow students to explore virtual environments, making complex subjects more accessible and engaging.

Case Study 5: Real Estate and Virtual Tours

- Real estate professionals are leveraging Vision Pro to offer virtual property tours. Clients can explore properties in a 3D space, experiencing the layout and design in a way that photos and videos cannot match.

Case Study 6: Retail and E-Commerce
- Vision Pro is transforming the retail experience by enabling virtual try-ons and showrooms. Customers can view products in 3D and make informed purchasing decisions without the need for physical samples.

These case studies demonstrate the versatility of the Apple Vision Pro and its potential to redefine professional practices across various sectors. As the device continues to evolve, it is likely to unlock even more applications that will shape the future of work and innovation.

Tips for Integrating Vision Pro into Your Workflow

Integrating the Apple Vision Pro into your professional workflow can significantly enhance productivity and creativity. Here are some tips to help you make the most of this innovative device:

- **Establish a Dedicated AR Workspace:** Designate a specific area in your office or home where you can use the Vision Pro without distractions. This will help you focus and fully immerse yourself in the AR environment.

- **Customize Your Virtual Interface:** Take advantage of Vision Pro's spatial interface to organize your virtual workspace. Place your most-used apps and tools within easy reach, and arrange additional screens as needed for multitasking.
- **Utilize Apple Pencil for Annotating:** The Apple Pencil can be a powerful tool for annotating documents and taking notes directly within the Vision Pro's interface. This can improve memory retention and streamline your note-taking process.
- **Leverage Spotlight Mode for Focus:** Activate Spotlight Mode to eliminate unnecessary stimuli and focus on the task at hand. This feature darkens everything except your primary window, allowing you to concentrate better.
- **Implement Smart Noise Reduction:** Use the Vision Pro's smart noise reduction feature to minimize background noise and distractions. This can be especially useful in busy environments or when you need to concentrate on audio-intensive tasks.

- **Sync with Other Apple Devices:** Ensure that your Vision Pro is synced with your other Apple devices for a seamless transition between them. This allows you to continue working on projects across different platforms while maintaining progress.
- **Schedule Regular Breaks:** Incorporate breaks into your schedule to prevent fatigue. The Vision Pro can remind you to take short breaks for stretching or movement, which is essential for maintaining productivity and health.
- **Explore Third-Party Apps and Tools:** Explore the App Store for third-party apps that can complement the Vision Pro's capabilities. Many developers are creating specialized tools that can enhance your workflow in various industries.
- **Stay Updated with Software Releases:** Keep your Vision Pro updated with the latest software releases to ensure you have access to new features and improvements that can benefit your workflow.
- **Participate in Community Forums:** Join online forums and communities dedicated to Vision Pro users. Sharing experiences and tips with other professionals can provide new insights

and help you discover innovative ways to use the device.

- **Provide Training for Team Members:** If you're implementing Vision Pro in a team setting, provide training for your colleagues to ensure everyone can effectively use the device. This will help maximize Vision Pro's benefits for your organization.

By following these tips, you can integrate the Apple Vision Pro into your professional workflow, unlocking new possibilities for efficiency, collaboration, and innovation.

Chapter 7

The Future of Vision Pro

Upcoming Features and Updates

The Apple Vision Pro, a groundbreaking device in the realm of spatial computing, continues to evolve. With each update, it brings new features that enhance the user experience and expand its capabilities. Here's a glimpse into the future of Vision Pro:

VisionOS Updates
- Apple is committed to regularly updating visionOS, ensuring that Vision Pro users have access to the latest advancements in spatial computing.
- Upcoming updates are expected to introduce new user interface enhancements, making navigation and interaction even more intuitive.

Enhanced 3D Camera Capabilities
- Future iterations of the Vision Pro will likely see improvements in the 3D camera system, offering even higher resolution and better depth sensing.
- These enhancements will allow for more detailed spatial photos and videos, providing users with richer content creation tools.

AI and Machine Learning Developments
- Apple's AI and machine learning features are set to become more sophisticated, providing users with personalized experiences that adapt to their habits and preferences.
- Anticipated updates may include more advanced facial recognition for security and personalized avatars, as well as smarter content recommendations.

Cross-Device Integration
- The integration between Vision Pro and other Apple devices is expected to deepen, with seamless synchronization and continuity features becoming more robust.
- Users can look forward to a more unified ecosystem where transferring tasks and data between devices is effortless.

Battery Life and Performance
- Apple is likely to focus on improving the battery life and overall performance of the Vision Pro, ensuring that users can enjoy longer sessions without the need for frequent charging.
- Advances in chip technology and power management will contribute to these improvements, making the Vision Pro even more convenient for professional and personal use.

Expanded App Ecosystem
- The Vision Pro's app ecosystem is set to grow, with developers creating new apps and tools specifically designed for spatial computing.
- These apps will take advantage of the device's unique capabilities, offering users a wider range of applications for work, creativity, and entertainment.

Accessibility Enhancements
- Apple is known for its commitment to accessibility, and the Vision Pro will continue to receive updates that make the device more inclusive for all users.
- Expect to see new features that cater to a broader range of needs, ensuring that everyone can experience the benefits of spatial computing.

The future of Apple Vision Pro is bright, with continuous innovation at its core. As the device matures, users can anticipate a stream of updates that will unlock new possibilities and redefine the way we interact with technology.

The Role of Vision Pro in the Future of Technology

The Apple Vision Pro is poised to play a pivotal role in the future of technology, shaping how we interact with the digital world. Here's an exploration of its potential impact:

Redefining Human-Computer Interaction
- Vision Pro's innovative interface, which relies on eye tracking and gestures, represents a significant shift from traditional input methods like keyboards and mice. This could lead to a more natural and intuitive way of interacting with computers, making technology more accessible and immersive.

Enhancing Decision-Making Processes
- By blending virtual reality (VR) and augmented reality (AR), Vision Pro has the potential to present new information and distill it from

existing environments, aiding in complex decision-making processes. This could transform industries by providing professionals with enhanced data visualization and situational awareness.

Driving the App Ecosystem Forward
- Apple's ecosystem of app developers is expected to expand with Vision Pro, as it offers a new platform for innovation. This could lead to the creation of applications that we haven't even imagined yet, further integrating AR into our daily lives.

Elevating Entertainment and Media
- With its high-resolution micro-OLED displays, Vision Pro is set to offer an unparalleled media consumption experience. This technology could revolutionize the entertainment industry, offering new ways to experience films, photos, and interactive content.

Influencing Social Connectivity
- Vision Pro's capabilities in creating hyper-realistic digital avatars and facilitating immersive communication could redefine social interactions. This might lead to a future where

digital presence feels as authentic as physical presence, altering how we connect with others.

Impacting Education and Training
- The immersive and interactive nature of Vision Pro makes it an ideal tool for education and training. It could provide students and professionals with experiential learning opportunities that enhance understanding and retention of complex concepts.

Shaping the Future of Work
- Vision Pro could transform the workplace by enabling virtual collaboration and remote work like never before. Its spatial computing power might allow teams to work together in virtual environments, regardless of their physical location.

Challenging Current Design Paradigms
- The design and functionality of Vision Pro challenge current paradigms, pushing the boundaries of what's possible with wearable technology. This could inspire a new wave of design thinking focused on user experience and environmental interaction.

Setting New Standards in Accessibility
- Apple's commitment to accessibility suggests that Vision Pro will continue to receive updates that make it more inclusive. This focus on accessibility could set new standards for technology design, ensuring that future devices are usable by everyone.

The Vision Pro is more than just a new device; it's a glimpse into the future of technology. Its impact is expected to be far-reaching, influencing how we live, work, and interact with the world around us.

Conclusion

The Apple Vision Pro represents a quantum leap in spatial computing and immersive experiences, blending cutting-edge augmented reality (AR) and virtual reality (VR) technologies into a single, powerful device. Throughout this comprehensive guide, we've explored the Vision Pro's extensive suite of capabilities, including:

- Seamless transitions between AR and VR modes for blending digital content with the physical world or complete virtual immersion.
- Exceptional visual fidelity with ultra-high-resolution displays and advanced rendering techniques for realistic virtual environments.
- Precise hand tracking and intuitive gesture controls for natural interactions with virtual objects and user interfaces.

- Spatial audio technology that maps sound in 3D space, creating an enveloping auditory experience.
- Robust environmental mapping and spatial awareness for anchoring virtual content accurately within real-world surroundings.
- Powerful authoring tools for creating and sharing immersive AR/VR experiences.
- Integrated productivity apps and collaboration features for efficient remote work and virtual meetings.
- Seamless integration with the broader Apple ecosystem for a cohesive cross-device experience.

With its cutting-edge features and capabilities, the Apple Vision Pro empowers users to explore new frontiers of creativity, learning, entertainment, and productivity, redefining the boundaries of immersive computing.

Future Possibilities and Potential Developments

As revolutionary as the Vision Pro is, it represents just the beginning of a new era in spatial computing. Apple's continued investment in research and development, combined with advances in hardware and software technologies, will undoubtedly fuel future iterations and enhancements to the Vision Pro platform.

Potential areas for future development include:

- Increased display resolution and field of view for even more immersive visual experiences.
- Advancements in eye-tracking and foveated rendering for improved visual performance and efficiency.
- Integration of advanced haptic feedback systems for enhanced tactile sensations within virtual environments.
- Further refinements in environmental mapping and object recognition are needed for more seamless AR/VR blending.
- Expanded ecosystem of third-party apps, games, and experiences tailored for the Vision Pro platform.
- Improved battery life and thermal management for extended usage sessions.
- Exploration of new input modalities, such as brain-computer interfaces, for more intuitive and natural interactions.

As the Vision Pro platform evolves, its potential applications will continue to expand, impacting fields as diverse as healthcare, engineering, education, and beyond. The possibilities are limitless, and Apple's commitment to pushing the boundaries of immersive computing will shape the future of how we interact with technology.

Resources for Further Learning and Support

To ensure you make the most of your Apple Vision Pro experience, Apple provides a comprehensive suite of resources for further learning and support:

Apple Support website: Access detailed user guides, troubleshooting articles, and FAQs related to the Vision Pro.

Apple Vision Pro Community Forums: Connect with other Vision Pro users, share tips and tricks, and get personalized support from Apple experts.

Apple Developer Resources: For developers, access comprehensive documentation, sample code, and tools for creating cutting-edge AR/VR apps and experiences for the Vision Pro.

Apple Retail Stores and Authorized Service Providers: Schedule in-person appointments or workshops to receive hands-on guidance and support from Apple's trained specialists.

Apple Vision Pro Online Courses: Enroll in interactive online courses covering various aspects of the Vision Pro, from beginner tutorials to advanced techniques.

Appendices

Glossary of Terms

Augmented Reality (AR): A technology that overlays digital information, objects, or environments onto the physical world, creating a composite view that blends virtual and real elements.

Environmental Mapping: The process of capturing and reconstructing the physical surroundings in digital form, enabling the precise positioning and integration of virtual content within real-world environments.

Eye Tracking: A sensor technology that monitors and tracks the movement and position of a user's eyes, enabling gaze-based interactions and optimized rendering.

Foveated Rendering: A rendering technique that allocates more processing power and resolution to the areas where the user's gaze is focused, improving visual quality and performance.

Gesture Recognition: The ability to interpret and respond to specific hand gestures and movements, enabling natural and intuitive interactions with virtual content.

Hand Tracking: A technology that precisely tracks the position, orientation, and movements of a user's hands, enabling direct manipulation of virtual objects.

Spatial Audio: Audio rendering techniques that simulate the way sound behaves in physical environments, creating an immersive and directional auditory experience.

Spatial Computing: A paradigm that integrates physical and digital spaces, enabling seamless interactions with virtual content within the context of the real world.

Virtual Reality (VR): A simulated, computer-generated environment that immerses the user in a fully digital experience, replacing their physical surroundings.

VisionOS: The operating system designed specifically for the Vision Pro, enabling spatial interactions and immersive experiences.

Digital Crown: A physical input mechanism on the Vision Pro, used for navigating the interface and adjusting settings.

Passthrough: A feature that uses the Vision Pro's cameras to allow users to see their surroundings while engaged in a virtual environment.

Accessibility Features and Settings

The Apple Vision Pro prioritizes accessibility, offering a range of features and settings to ensure an inclusive and accommodating experience for users with varying needs and abilities. Key accessibility options include:

Vision:
- Display accommodations (zoom, contrast, color filters)
- Text-to-speech and audio descriptions
- Head tracking for cursor control

Hearing:
- Customizable audio settings (volume, equalization)

- Visual alerts and indicators
- Support for hearing aids and cochlear implants

Motor Skills:
- Voice control and dictation
- Switch control for alternative input methods
- Adjustable gesture sensitivity and controls

Safety Guidelines and Best Practices

While the Vision Pro offers immersive and engaging experiences, it's crucial to prioritize safety and well-being during extended usage sessions. Key safety guidelines include:

- Take regular breaks to avoid eye strain, fatigue, and discomfort.
- Maintain spatial awareness of your physical surroundings to prevent collisions or accidents.
- Ensure proper ventilation and hydration to mitigate potential motion sickness.
- Adjust display settings (brightness, contrast, IPD) for optimal visual comfort.
- Adhere to age restrictions and consult healthcare professionals for photosensitive conditions.
- Maintain proper posture and ergonomics to prevent muscle strain and injury.

Warranty and Support Information

Apple Vision Pro Limited Warranty:
- Covers defects in materials and workmanship for one year from the date of purchase.
- Includes technical support and service at Apple Retail Stores or Authorized Service Providers.
- Excludes coverage for normal wear and tear, misuse, or unauthorized modifications.

Extended AppleCare+ Protection Plan (optional):
- Extends warranty coverage and provides up to two incidents of accidental damage protection.
- Includes priority access to Apple experts and technical support resources.
- Available for purchase at the time of device purchase or within 60 days.

Support Resources:
- Apple Support website (www.apple.com/support/vision-pro)
- Vision Pro Community Forums
- Apple Retail Store appointments and workshops
- Online user guides and troubleshooting documentation

About the Author

William C. Wills is a renowned technology expert and author who is passionate about demystifying complex devices and empowering users to unlock their full potential. With a career spanning over two decades in the tech industry, he has established himself as a trusted voice in the fields of consumer electronics and smart home automation.

Born in Silicon Valley, the epicenter of technological innovation, William was exposed to the ever-evolving world of gadgets and gizmos from a young age. This early exposure ignited a lifelong fascination with technology and a desire to make it accessible to everyone, regardless of their technical expertise.

After graduating from Stanford University with a degree in Computer Science, William embarked on a journey that took him to the forefront of the tech industry. He worked with leading companies, contributing to the development of cutting-edge products and services that revolutionized the way we live and interact with technology.

www.ingramcontent.com/pod-product-compliance
Lightning Source LLC
Chambersburg PA
CBHW070408230526
45471CB00006B/2701